Shanghai Posters
The Power of Advertising

Published by:
FormAsia Books Limited
706, Yu Yuet Lai Building
45, Wyndham Street
Central, Hong Kong
www.formasiabooks.com

Published 2005
ISBN: 962-7283-95-9

Text and photographs © FormAsia Books Limited

Written by Anna Hestler, Hong Kong
Editorial Assistance – Peter Moss, Hong Kong
Edited by James Cox; Tai Peng Editing, Lamma Island
Art Direction – Hans Lindberg, Vaucluse, France
Photography – Sathish Gobinath, Hong Kong
Digital Artwork – Kitty Chan, Hong Kong
FormAsia Marketing – Eliza Lee, Hong Kong

Source of Posters
Honeychurch Antiques – Hong Kong
Wing Tai Curios Centre – Macau
ChinaArt – Hong Kong

Printed in Hong Kong
Printed by Sing Cheong Printing Company Ltd.
Film separations by Sky Art Graphic Company Ltd.

Rights reserved.
Reproduction permitted on written permission of
FormAsia Books Limited.

SHANGHAI
Posters

Anna Hestler

FormAsia

Portraits of a generation

Women took on a whole new image in advertising during Shanghai's 'belle' epoch. In the early twentieth century, advertisers combined images of beautiful women with everyday products to create an advertising medium that broke with artistic and social tradition – the 'beautiful lady' calendar poster. The ladies became the faces of dreams, and proved to be so persuasive that the products advertised became secondary in the design of the posters. The story of the calendar poster is directly linked to the birth of modern Shanghai, the influx of western ideas and the culture of consumerism that followed.

Translated, 'Shanghai' means 'above the sea' – a name that could not be more appropriate, as the city rose above every other to become China's brightest star. From the mid-nineteenth century until the Second World War, Shanghai was China's economic miracle and cultural trendsetter. In its heyday, it produced most of the country's manufactured goods, and had so many film studios that it was dubbed the 'Hollywood of the East'. It was a place where the Occident and the Orient collided to create a modern economy, a liberal society and a vibrant culture.

Shanghai was thrust into the international limelight after China's defeat in the first Opium War. Under the Treaty of Nanking (1842) Shanghai and four other ports were opened to foreign trade, and Britain was granted a slew of privileges including exemption from Chinese Imperial law. Shanghai immediately became the leading treaty port, and the new base for British and American opium and cotton traders. Foreign settlements sprang up along the banks of the muddy Whangpu River, which would later become the finest Bund – or waterfront settlement – in the world.

As a thriving trading centre and enclave protected by foreign diplomats and gunboats, Shanghai had no trouble attracting a limitless supply of cheap labour. Peasants fleeing rural poverty and hardship flocked to the city to become human beasts of burden. When the Taiping Rebellion broke out in 1850, thousands of Chinese refugees poured into Shanghai carrying rice pots, bedding, birdcages and all their portable wealth. The price of land on the Bund shot up from $200 per acre to $50,000, and a spectacular building boom ensued. Along the Bund, the foundations for magnificent colonial edifices such as the HongKong and Shanghai Bank were laid by coolies who sweated and staggered under backbreaking loads for subsistence wages.

Created from both Chinese and foreign capital, the HongKong and Shanghai Bank was a symbol of how East and West came together to build modern Shanghai.

It was only through the assistance of their Chinese managers, or *compradors*, that the *taipans*, as the heads of foreign firms were called, gained access to Chinese labour, loans from native banks and capital from wealthy merchants and officials from the delta cities.

By 1870, Shanghai had become the world's fifth largest trading port, and China's commercial and financial centre. Following China's defeat in the Sino-Japanese War in 1895, Japan also became a treaty power and began to build factories in Shanghai. Spurred on by the competition, the British, Germans and Chinese followed suit. Windowless red-brick factories soon transformed the landscape; cotton, paper and textile mills; chemical, tobacco and match factories mushroomed along the banks of the Whangpu River and Soochow Creek. Shanghai had become an international centre of commerce, finance and industry.

By 1910, the city was a cosmopolitan metropolis of a million souls. It was, in fact, comprised of three cities, each governed by separate laws and administrations. The only one of the three directly subordinate to Peking was the Chinese municipality, a compact and crowded quarter where people hurried through narrow, twisting lanes past steaming food stalls and dimly lit shops on their way to the teahouse or temple. Beyond the Chinese city lay the leafy avenues and western-style mansions of the French Concession, which the French Government referred to as 'un petit pièce de la France'. The third city – the International Settlement – was the wealthiest and most modern part of Shanghai, formed when the Americans joined forces with the British settlement in 1863. By the 1930s, it was home to citizens of over 60 countries. There were German Jews, Parsee merchants, Filipino sailors, White Russian princes and countesses who had fled the revolution in their homeland; and bearded Sikhs who served as the settlement's police force.

Migration into Shanghai was constant, and the city's population grew continually. While a minority lived a life of riches and excitement, most of Shanghai's residents eked out a living and called Dickensian slums home. Men laboured to the point of exhaustion, while women and children worked their fingers to the bone in dimly lit factories for up to sixteen hours a day. Beggars with missing limbs were sprawled across the pavement, and prostitutes of all races roamed the streets. Every day special carts collected the corpses of the poor souls who had died in the alleys and gutters of China's richest city. Unemployment, strikes and glaring social ills made Shanghai a breeding ground for revolutionary politics. In 1921, the Communist Party was formed in the French Concession, only to be driven underground by Chiang Kai-shek's massacre of hundreds – perhaps thousands – of strikers on 12 April 1927. Six days later, Chiang declared a new government in Nanking, sparking a twenty-year rivalry between the Nationalists and the Communists. His marriage to Soong Mei-ling, the daughter of a well-to-do industrialist, secured his ties with Shanghai's wealthy Chinese and foreigners.

Throughout most of the 20s and 30s, a secret society known as the Green Gang ruled Shanghai's underworld. The Green Gang's power base was its monopoly of the opium trade, and its leader's long, brown-stained fingernails revealed his own addiction. Shopkeepers, restaurateurs and factory owners were forced to pay protection money to the gangsters, and wealthy Chinese were occasionally kidnapped for ransom. The Green Gang had excellent connections with Shanghai's foreign and Chinese authorities and the Gang ensured they would remain excellent – and that its illicit trade in drugs, prostitution, extortion and kidnapping would remain secure – by distributing an estimated twenty million dollars in bribes each year.

Shanghai soaked up foreign ideas of all sorts and the cosmopolitan city became the nation's trendsetter. Its theatres – the Lyceum, Grand, Empire, Odeon and Apollo – were as grand as New York's, and its cinemas often showed Hollywood films before they were released in America. By 1920, there were over one hundred film companies in Shanghai; and until 1949, when the communists arrived, major American motion picture studios such as MGM had offices in the city. Newspaper, magazine and book publishing blossomed then boomed, and the city's printing presses churned out highbrow literature, gossip magazines and everything in between. In 'Culture-Street', serious bookworms could find anything from European classics – in their original languages or Chinese translation – to Chinese comics.

Shanghai's affluent and sophisticated Chinese elite adopted many western ideas, and many soon became conspicuous consumers in the western style. Chinese tycoons lived in mock – Tudor villas with swimming pools, tennis courts and English-style gardens, and travelled by chauffeur-driven Daimlers and Isotta-Fraschinis. In time, social barriers broke down and East and West became entwined. Chinese businessmen in trousers and satin shirts sipped cocktails with dapper British gents. Socialites such as Mrs Chester

Fritz – a striking Hungarian Jewess – held sumptuous dinner parties where Chinese financiers, politicians and artists mixed with distinguished members of foreign society. It wasn't long before Chinese wives and daughters – decent and modest women – began making their appearances at dinner parties and nightclubs. They came out like shy debutantes carrying gold and enamel compacts. Soon they were smoking, drinking, dancing the Charleston at the Astor House Hotel tea dances and shopping at American-style department stores.

The arrival of the department store ushered in the modern era of consumerism in Shanghai. People no longer relied on personal relationships with shopkeepers; instead they relied on the reputation of brand-name products. In 1917, the Sincere Company brought the first department store with American-style merchandising to Nanking Road. Wing On, Sun Sun and the Sun Companies appeared soon after, together they became known as the

'Big Four'. Their emporiums were packed with a staggering array of Chinese and foreign merchandise, as well as restaurants, theatres and elaborate rooftop gardens with tables for tea. The department store fuelled a desire for material possessions and introduced the western notion: you are what you own.

Other western ideas such as concepts of equality between the sexes were also influential, leading to the birth of the women's liberation movement in 1898. Its supporters called for the sweeping away of traditional Chinese practices that impeded women's freedom. Girl's schools which advocated equality and independence for women were established. Here girls were taught to read and write, and they were encouraged to play sport, a pursuit previously thought to be unfeminine.

After the founding of the Republic of China in 1911, Shanghai became the heart of the women's liberation movement, and its women the vanguards of the modern age with their clarion call of 'Rise, sisters! Rise!'. Gradually, more women entered the workforce as bank tellers, typists, sales clerks and telephone operators. As their purchasing power increased, women set their sights on more than marriage and motherhood. They adopted the glamorous film stars of Hollywood and Shanghai's film industry as their role models and dreamt of modern appliances that would free them from domestic drudgery.

As consumerism gained momentum, foreign and Chinese companies competed fiercely for market dominance. Foreign merchants began using imported posters with pictures of western personalities, scenery and religious imagery to advertise their products, but these failed to attract the attention of the consumer. They responded by featuring Chinese paintings in their posters, which were aesthetically pleasing but lacked punch as advertisements. Realising that they needed to modify their advertising, foreign merchants turned to the calendar poster.

Calendar posters or *yuefenpai* are representative of China's earliest commercial art, and were part of a larger body of Chinese folk art that featured traditional Chinese New Year pictures. These folk prints depicted human and divine figures, legends and operatic stories, flowers, birds, and landscapes, and were printed with both lunar and solar calendars. Calendar posters were being used for advertising as early as 1896 when the Shanghai Hong Fu Lai Lottery Company began handing out complimentary copies with the purchase of lottery tickets. However, it wasn't until foreign companies modified the traditional, rather staid calendar poster and appropriated it as a medium for directly advertising their goods that the posters took their first steps towards becoming a ubiquitous phenomenon.

Conscious of the need to appeal to local tastes, foreign merchants approached famous folk painters such as Zhou Muqiao, Zhao Ousheng and Li Shaozhang to help commercialise calendar posters. These painters managed to blend the techniques of traditional Chinese paintings with New Year pictures in a way that met the requirements of advertising. At first, the posters were simple advertisements that featured only foreign products. It was only when beautiful women began to adorn the images that the posters really caught the public's eye. People began referring to them as *meinu yuefenpai* or 'beautiful lady' calendar posters, and a whole new genre of advertising posters was born.

The women became the selling point, and as a result, the products being advertised were often inconspicuously positioned on the sidelines to ensure that they did not detract from the main attraction. The women were shown alone, together and with their children; and they fell into two categories: classical beauties of ancient China, and modern-day women of the Republic. As Chinese society became more liberal, advertisers began employing film stars as models. As the highest paid performer in the film industry Butterfly Wu, or Hue Die, never failed to command attention, and the voluptuous dimpled beauty appeared on many posters of the 20s and 30s. The women in the calendar posters epitomised the perfect female, both in form and human spirit, and were painted with exquisite detail. Since figure painting required great skill, a division of labour was instituted to utilise the specific talents of the artists. The master painter was responsible for painting the human figures, while apprentices and less-skilled painters created the background and the products being advertised. In painting the women, the masters tried to attain the effect of *hua jin yi zai* or 'finished paintings with lingering emotions', an artistic philosophy that stemmed from a longstanding tradition of Chinese portraiture.

The aesthetics of calendar art were particularly important. According to Chinese tradition, a woman must be lovely and elegant; and her hairstyle and clothing must reflect this. Every strand of hair was meticulously painted, and decorative items of clothing were matched to show harmony and style. Even the garment's folds and creases were painted to emphasise the beauty of an elegant pose.

Beauty was paramount, and the woman's appearance had to depict her character and mood. The eyes were a focal point and were always painted first, providing a window to the subject's soul. The eyelids and eyebrows were painted next, followed by the nose, mouth, facial contours, ears, hair, hands and clothes. Like the eyes, the hands were also a focal point, thought to be an expression of a woman's disposition. The hands of beautiful women were painted in various positions: elegantly extended, demurely crossed, gracefully curved, and so on. Even the background of the poster was thoughtfully chosen to reflect the subject's mood. The four seasons and elements of weather such as rain, fog and sunset glows were all used to convey the ebb and flow of a woman's emotions.

Chinese painters adopted western techniques to make their paintings more life-like in their quest to portray perfect female beauty. They abandoned traditional approaches to Chinese painting, such as strong contours and flat colourwash, and turned to western perspective painting and watercolours. Influential artists such as Zheng Mantuo developed new painting techniques that laid the foundations of a distinctive style in calendar posters. His rub-and-dub method involved rubbing carbon powder over the image and then applying watercolours to create a natural rosy complexion. It added depth and a new realism. With western painting techniques, the artists were able to bring the women to life through more vivid facial expressions and postures. The public loved this and the artists exploited the potential of these new techniques to the fullest.

While calendar posters featured an array of products, by far the most avid exploiters of this advertising medium were the tobacco companies. Advertising wars raged between giants such as the British-American Tobacco Company (BAT) and the Nanyang Tobacco Company, as they fought to establish brand dominance. In doing so, they targeted women with advertisements that showed females smoking. Some claimed that smoking was sexy; others linked it to happiness; but all associated smoking with a modern and bourgeois lifestyle. Other items featured in calendar posters included beauty products such as face powders and creams; Chinese and Western medicines; foodstuffs such as cola, beer and baby food; and domestic appliances. These posters of beautiful women became such an effective advertising medium that even fertiliser companies began using them – and no one batted an eye.

The women in the calendar posters performed far more than the function of advertising products. They helped redefine the role of women and set trends in female fashion. In them, independent women posed at leisure, in fashionable clothes and, on occasion, even *déshabillé*. They were progressive women who enjoyed foreign sports such as golf, tennis and horseback riding. They were the first to wear *qipaos* that had shorter hemlines and were tailored to accentuate the waist. They wore western-style evening gowns and created a hybrid style of East and West. A popular look of the era was the traditional *qipao* combined with a western overcoat, and accessories such as stoles of mink and fox fur.

Calendar posters provide a revealing glimpse of Shanghai society during the 20s and 30s. Apart from the beautiful ladies, the posters were manifestations of society's desire for prosperity and urban life. Behind the beautiful women and new products were swanky home furnishings, dance halls, sandy beaches, tennis courts and other dreamy settings. In short, the posters were a reflection of what society wanted to become. They were portraits of an illusionary era; but it was an era in its final act.

With the start of China's War of Resistance against Japan in 1937, China's industry and commerce went into decline. Then, on 14 August 1937, disaster struck. Chinese pilots attempting to strike a Japanese flagship accidentally dropped several bombs over the Bund and some of the busiest parts of the city. Three thousand people were killed or injured. Panic seized the city. Shop fronts were boarded up and business came to a standstill. The British Consulate General staff fled from their office, and all the banks along the Bund locked their doors. To the terror-stricken population it must have appeared that the British were fleeing Shanghai.

By December 1937, the Japanese had occupied the Chinese parts of Shanghai. Surrounded on all sides, Shanghai's western concessions – often referred to as the 'lonely island' – weathered the storm for a short period and calendar posters continued to be produced with foreign funds. The outbreak of the Second World War in September 1939 forced Britain to withdraw its troops from the port, and foreign governments began evacuating women and children. When the Japanese bombed Pearl Harbour on 7 December 1941, Shanghai ceased to be a treaty port and the foreign concessions were occupied by the Japanese. It was the end of a world of dreams. Artists were forced to paint calendar posters for the Japanese and the models in the posters became increasingly Japanese looking. Some artists used the posters to express political messages about the occupation, and works with themes such as *Heaven and Hell* and *The Ten Kings of Purgatory* appeared. Some pre-war calendar posters were smuggled out of the city, only to re-emerge almost 80 years later in modern Shanghai.

The city was liberated in 1945 and lived in a strange limbo during the civil war between the Nationalists and the Communists until it fell to the Red Army in 1949. Calendar posters experienced a revival in the early days of the People's Republic of China, and were used to advertise products made by cooperatives. The posters took on a completely new look and the themes became patriotic. Pictures of women who wore drab green military uniforms and caps with red stars replaced the glamorous beauties so loved by Shanghai society. In time, the posters no longer carried advertising messages, but were used to communicate the Chinese Communist Party's vision to the illiterate masses.

During the Cultural Revolution (1966-1976), calendar posters were used exclusively for the propagation of political slogans such as 'Long Live Chairman Mao' and messages extorting peasants and workers to give their utmost to the communist cause. Many aspects of everyday life came under attack. Shopkeepers no longer carried western-style clothing, and women stopped wearing western-style hairdos. In bookshops, Mao's 'Little Red Book' replaced novels and magazines. As the propaganda of the Red Guards reached its climax, members of the intelligentsia were labelled as reactionaries and thousands of 'beautiful lady' calendar posters were confiscated and burned – Shanghai's beautiful ladies and a generation's dreams went up in smoke.

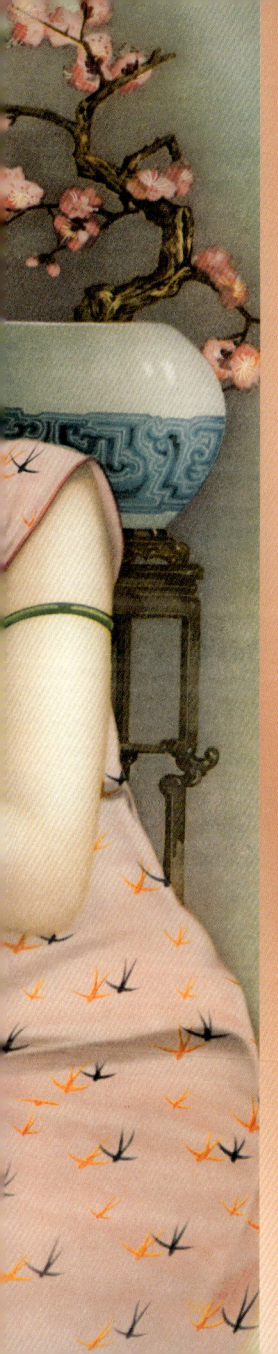

They were young, of good parentage, admired and courted in the select circles of the social elite. The richly provided life they led flowed like an endlessly serene river. How could they know that it wouldn't – all too soon – reach its end in a tumultuous sea?

While some models oozed sex appeal, others were depicted with plump children. Chubby offspring, having long symbolised wealth and prosperity in traditional China, still carried those credentials in the Shanghai of thirties.

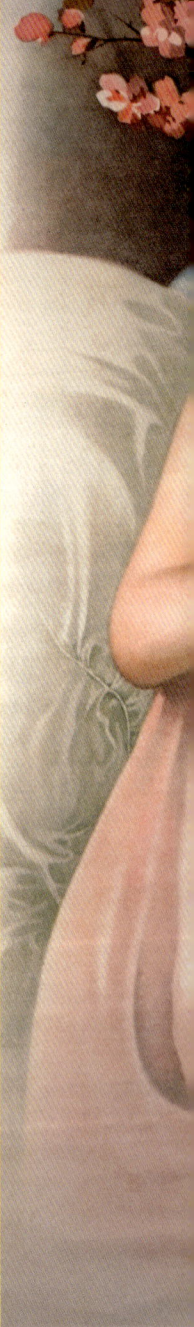

However desirable the attributes of the lifestyle in which they portrayed their idealised role models, the artists of these unique vignettes of thirties Shanghai would frequently remind viewers of the paramount importance of motherhood. No matter how modern they might strive to appear, the young women of Shanghai still had the sacred duty to raise the next generation who would populate this seemingly unassailably prosperous city.

Chinese distillers quickly followed the newest trends in advertising with posters of Parrot Wine, which promised respite from boredom through wine, women and song.

In 1923, Lever Bros launched Lux Toilet Soap in Shanghai. Through a concerted advertising campaign that stressed luxury and glamour, the company built a brand still popular in modern-day China.

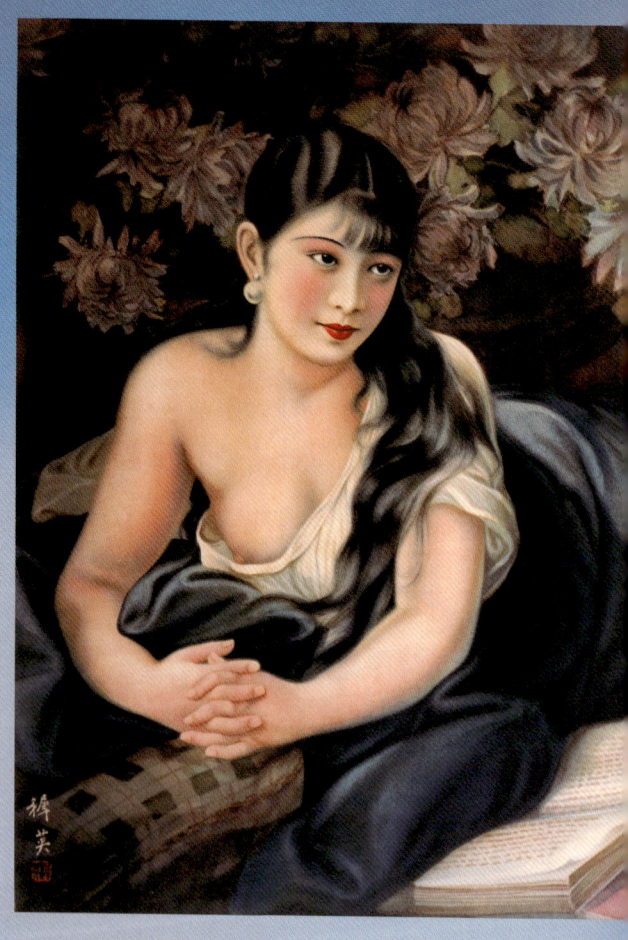

Many of Shanghai's artists studied in Europe and returned to China with a new vision of the ideal woman. They combined Eastern and Western standards of beauty to create fictitious

goddesses with shiny black hair and sensuous curves. Shanghai 'calendar girls' were intended to embody the modern Chinese woman, self-consciously imitating European artists.

Shanghai's early industrial forays provided a living not only for those manufacturing soaps, powders, lingerie, torches and other export goods but also for the artists commissioned to create alluring posters and package designs.

The Great Eastern Dispensary offered Chinese and Western medicine under the brand name *Wanxiang* (everlasting prosperity). Two prime products were Pink Pills for pale people and Baby Face cream for ladies.

The forerunner of today's global chain of the 'Body Shop', offered Shanghainese herbal creams, balms, oils and scented salts in the eternal pursuit of youthfulness.

Faced with stiff competition, the Nanyang Tobacco Company encouraged consumers to boycott foreign manufactured cigarettes. Advertisements for the Ngaikuo (patriot) brand took the line that, 'If one cherishes one's country, one should only smoke Ngaikuo brand cigarettes.'

Some calendar posters were bulk produced, then pre-sold to a variety of manufacturers who in turn overprinted their products either in the foreground or background of the image. Printers were known to reward loyal clients with posters of languid, provocatively posed women as gifts for Chinese New Year.

Calendar models broke with tradition and established a new ethic that effectively rejected the Confucian virtue of sexual modesty. They exposed more than had ever been portrayed anywhere in China other than in rare private collections of erotic art.

Created by Fung Fook, and inspired by 'two angels' he saw walking hand in hand, the Girl Brand was used to promote a line of toiletries including perfume, tooth powder and vanishing cream.

Shanghai pioneered a movie world all its own, spiced with sex and glamour. Entrepreneurs went to great lengths to out-dazzle their competitors,

and project an image of style, class and sophistication, regularly featuring glamorous film stars in their commercial promotions.

Early advertisements for China's Ka Wah Bank (still in business today) attempted to persuade patrons to place their earnings in the security of a savings account, rather than conceal cash under Grandmother's mattress.

Hu Die (Butterfly Wu), was the most celebrated Chinese film actress in the twenties and thirties. Her multitude of fans in Shanghai 'felt she belonged to them'. They queued up to see her light up the screen. Gossip about her sold newspapers and manufacturers clamoured for her endorsement to promote their products.

A fan of ostrich feathers was just the thing to set off an outfit and underscore a woman's grace, good looks and social standing. Revered by an adoring Shanghai public, 'Butterfly Wu' (below) embellishes the package of a soap manufacturer.

The desire for a pale complexion has a long history in China. In their early efforts to lighten up, aristocratic women ground pearls into fine powder which they swallowed in the firm belief that it would whiten their complexion. In Shanghai of the thirties, the means may have proved defunct but the end was still a worthy objective.

The Eveready Company took on the daunting task of lighting up Shanghai. Their torches were renowned, but finding their batteries for sale in thirties Shanghai remained a challenge.

In his early years, poster artist Zhen Mantao hawked paintings of delicate classic Chinese faces in the side streets off Nanking Road. One day a renowned cosmetic manufacturer discovered and bought his fine renderings. News of Zhen's achievement spread so rapidly that his reputation rocketed to fame.

Some three decades before western counterparts launched their sexual revolution, Shanghai women displayed an air of confidence that betokened their own quiet liberation. Neither aggressive nor overstated, it was nevertheless apparent in their self-assurance, their deportment, the attitudes they struck. In this exuberant metropolis they were courted, admired and pampered.

柏福
名馳界世爐此
ES

福柏士打汽爐乃市上最
佳之打汽爐製造堅固一
無爆烈之危險用火油極
省非常經濟推火力偉大

Shanghai's calendar posters are still much sought after by international art collectors. The highest prices are fetched by advertisements which carry a company name still in existence today, as well as the name of the original artist.

打士柏福

Women who couldn't afford off-the-peg fashions, modelled on Shanghai posters, sought to achieve miracles with needle, thread and knitting wool. Canny continental tailors offered them sewing courses patterned on the latest European styles.

By 1928, the Chinese "flapper" was turning heads on Shanghai streets. One newspaper reported, "She is usually dressed in semi-foreign style with bobbed hair and short skirt... and powdered face. She attends movies regularly and expects to be courted in screen lover fashion." (The North China Herald)

While in some ways calendar posters exploited women as sex objects, they also celebrated their freedom from the shackles of domestic drudgery. But though they

offered idealised beacons of female modernity, such overt representations of liberation hardly reflected the reality of thirties Shanghai.

As early as 1819, tin cans were manufactured for marketing products ranging from biscuits and confectionery to cosmetics. This revolutionary concept was practical and often treasured for storing miscellaneous items long after the original contents were consumed.

Tobacco advertisers encouraged women to light up by associating smoking with the lifestyle of the professional woman. Prominent singers, dance hostesses, film stars and others who led independent and free-spirited lives were the exemplars of this brave and bold new world.

製造元 明治牛乳公司

3 LBS. NET
BABY'S SAFEST FOOD
MILCOGEN
REGISTERED
WORLDWIDE WELLKNOWN
AN IDEAL POWDERED
WHOLE MILK FOR INFANTS
AND NURSING MOTHERS
PREPARED BY
MEIJI DAIRY PRODUCTS CO.,LTD.

MILCOG

世界最優秀的！

"美兒固精"代乳粉

Another new-fangled western invention to Shanghai was powdered baby milk. It must initially have come both as a surprise and a blessing to socially preoccupied Chinese mothers, who would never have imagined such a peculiarly ingenious product could replace the traditional suckling services offered by a hired baby *amah*.

Madame Garnet's was the most exclusive dress salon in Shanghai. Blond, with a ballerina's body, the White Russian owner was known to refuse to tailor clothes for women exceeding her standards for acceptable anatomical dimensions that verged on avoirdupois.

In the Russian restaurants on Shanghai's Avenue Joffre, frequented by writers, artists, and photographers, one could order soup, a main dish and endless cups of tea for just twenty cents – 24 hours round the clock.

As if emulating an aquatic variation on Botticelli's *Primavera*, naiad-like Chinese maidens cavort in transparent diaphanous

gowns around a reclining nymph in this waterborne reverie that offers tribute to an oriental *Spring.*

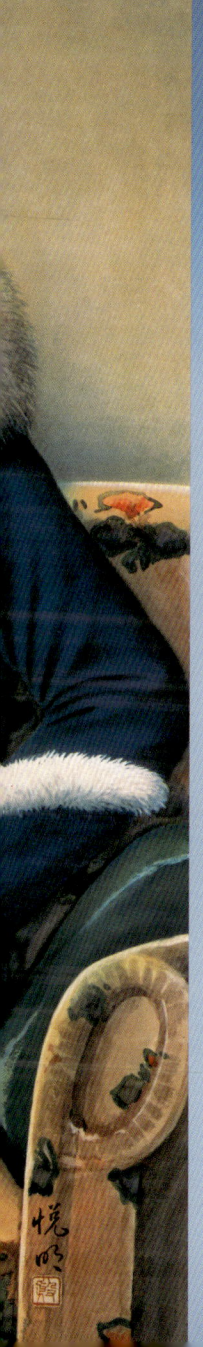

Early calendar posters depicted women in the traditional, conservative dress of the Qing Dynasty (1644–1911). After the fall of the Manchus, western taste became the vogue, revolutionising the fashions that swept through the more outward-looking cities of Shanghai, Canton and Hong Kong.

Trademarked in 1893, John Player & Sons' familiar logo of a rustic, bearded sailor in the prime of life made Navy Cut cigarettes into a top-selling brand, sweeping aside whatever competition was offered by such labels as "Three Flags", "My Dear" and "The Rat".

Many Chinese painters designed trademarks for companies such as Wilkinson, Heywood & Clark. Some artists owned their own printing presses, allowing them total control over the entire calendar-making process, from design and artistic creativity to production-line output.

Shanghai in its roaring thirties was an amazing spectacle, reverberating in the western imagination as a place of style, excitement and intrigue. Yet in traditional Chinese society a woman's place tended to remain in the seclusion of the home. Though no longer wrapped in embroidered silks and swaying on bound feet, she was enlightened enough to pursue lifestyles reflecting the aspirations of Shanghai's rising middle class.

The cheongsam, a one piece, close-fitting garment with a stiff round collar and slit to the thigh, easy to slip on and comfortable to wear, enjoyed growing popularity in the international world of thirties Shanghai. Known as *'long dress'* in China's southern provinces or *'qipao'* in the north, the garment had its origins in Manchu rule. Although the 1911 Revolution toppled the domination of the Qing (Manchu) Dynasty, the cheongsam survived the stigma of political change to become formal attire for Chinese women.

By the thirties, Shanghai had everything a woman dreamed of. Downtown Nanking Road showcased the accoutrements of a by now increasingly global modernity. At Sincere and Wing On Department stores (still in business today), one could buy French cosmetics, Japanese kimonos and delicately embroidered Chinese lingerie.

German pharmaceutical company, Höchst, another company that remains in business today, used an oriental version of 'the girl next door,' to promote its health tonic in Shanghai. Its advertising slogan was to the point, suggesting that the more iron there was in the blood, the greater the vigour infusing the body.

Of all China's cities, Shanghai was the one its women most coveted, the centre of their country's thrust into the modern age, the pearl in its oyster. If not the best of all possible worlds, it certainly represented the best of all available worlds. To live there was to know that their time had come.

Shanghai was progressive and audacious in everything from dress to politics. By the beginning of the twentieth century, its women had cast off their loose-fitting *quipaos* and were advocating women's rights.

Engaged in passionate discussion on topics ranging from Marxism to free love, Shanghai poster artists could be found frequenting the smoke-filled tea houses and coffee shops of north Szechuan Road or in the Victory and Lear Bars in the Western Concessions.

Perfumers and fine soap makers to the Prince of Wales, Yardley sold a soothing range of products in China including talc powder, the most popular scent being English lavender.

Shanghai wedding attire was as much a Chinese as a Western creation. Brides wore the auspicious red satin *kwa*, but modified with a gauze veil rather than the traditional tasseled phoenix coronet.

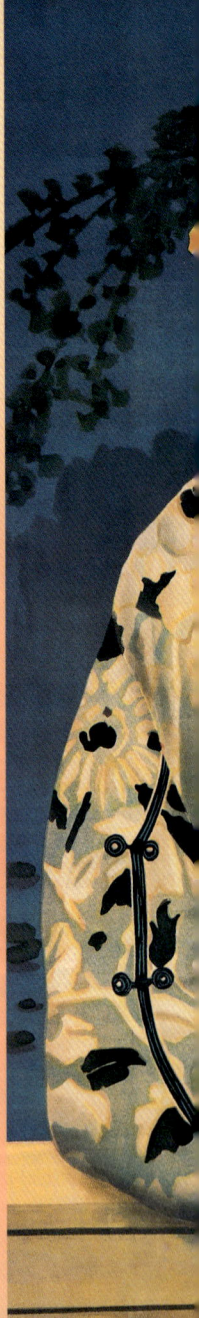

At the beginning of the twentieth century, foreign merchants and printing houses imported advanced printing machinery, making it possible to mass produce calendar posters by lithography.

In a society woman, intellect was almost as desirable an attribute as appearance. And it need be suggested by nothing more conspicuous than a book in the hand or a hint of dreamy aspiration in the eye.

No activity was more liberating to the Chinese female form than indulgence in the more risqué pursuits introduced by the West, such as disporting oneself in beach attire or riding a bicycle.

Keeping fit was an especially novel concept of the thirties lifestyle in Shanghai. Women were introduced to archery, golf lessons and tennis and even went horseback riding. Some joined the Circle Sportif, a French-run sporting and social club that admitted female members.

To raise the next generation of equally lovely maidens who would grace the ballrooms, tennis lawns and bathing beaches of the rich and the celebrated was the ambition of most society women. Elsewhere in China, boys would be the most desirable offspring, but Shanghai mothers knew better who would receive the greatest attention in maturity.

Swimsuit models made a big splash in 1909, when the YWCA opened the first pool that admitted Chinese. Although at first as modest as bathing attire in the West, Shanghai swimwear became ever more slinky and chic, adding a further touch of glamour to the city's aquatic pursuits.

Images of shot putters were copied from newspaper photos of the Berlin Olympics (1936), stressing the importance of physical fitness for girls.

"Oh dear! Another day! What's on the agenda? A picnic, a boating excursion, a garden party, another day at the races? Just as I was looking forward to reading a few more pages of the latest fashion magazine. Ah well, let me reach for my rouge and my powder, and fetch me my outdoor trousseau, with perhaps a single rope of pearls."

In Shanghai's Sing Song houses, elegant ladies entertained their clientele by singing, reciting poetry and playing musical instruments well into the following morning.

When the Nationalist government came to power in 1938, left-wing artists and intellectuals slipped into the French Concession or the International Settlement to escape censorship. Those who supported communist causes lived in fear of persecution, imprisonment or even torture.

Comrade Jiang Ching, better known as Madame Mao, transformed revolutionary ballet into a propaganda vehicle, redirecting the talents of thirties Shanghai artists to an official toeing of the Party line. The very names of the various ballets were redolent with revolution. 'Taking Tiger Mountain by Strategy', 'Raid on White Tiger Regiment' and 'Red Detachment of Women'.

When the Red Army crossed the Yangtze River in June 1949, Shanghai fell to the communists. The hues of artist's pallets turned predominantly red as they knuckled down to replace eulogies to the female form with Party propaganda under the authority of the Shanghai Art Publishing House.

During the Cultural Revolution (1966-1978), 'entertainment' was considered bourgeois decadence. Revolutionary ballet however, as in 'The Landlord', here being vilified by the Red Detachment of Women, was deemed appropriate. Entertainment became a 'proletarian statement'.

On seizing power in Shanghai in 1949, The Communist Party utilised the propaganda potential of women to further its message of Mao's class struggle. *"All our literature and art are for the masses of the people and in the first place for the workers, peasants and soldiers."* Quotation from Chairman Mao.